I
do not know

why it took so much time

for me...

Dr. Gopal

WestBow
P R E S S
A DIVISION OF THOMAS NELSON

WestBow Press books may be ordered through booksellers or by contacting:

WestBow Press
A Division of Thomas Nelson
1663 Liberty Drive
Bloomington, IN 47403
www.westbowpress.com
1-(866) 928-1240

ISBN: 978-1-4497-6270-4 (sc)

Library of Congress Control Number: 2012914180

Printed in the United States of America

WestBow Press rev. date: 10/05/2012

Respectfully Dedicated To

My Parents

Smt. Lalitha Viswanathan

Sri. M.M.Viswanathan

Contents

PREFACE

The humanity accumulates lifelong experiences as they pass thru a life cycle and these are rich resources of diamond mines. The humanity keeps all these invaluable resources to themselves and eventually ends up with their life time.

My personal opinion is that these experiences are rich untapped resource for the forthcoming generations while, the young generations go thru the same kind of Don'ts and misbehaviors and end up with the same loop of problems what the previous generations have gone through. In today's world we see the younger generation has very disturbed mind set which is very obvious from the recent Tucson, AZ incident and similar such incidents. When such a group of disturbed minds come together, eventually nucleates global terrorism. Even in the 9/11 incident most of the accused were misdirected youths. We have gone through several such massacres in the modern era. All these are happening because the younger generations absolutely do not have the consciousness of their purpose and responsibilities.

My opinion is that the educated world has the responsibility of teaching and directing the youth force in the productive direction. The lack of knowledge and the misbehavior of these youths lead to heavy tragedies. There are a lot of evil forces around this world, who are ready to take advantage of this situation, mislead the youth community. The main reason is lack of understanding of life and improper information received from various rotten sources. The rotten sources have understood their weak and agitated minds and influence them to their tune.

If the younger generations understand the value of their life and keep looking deeper in to themselves and fix their problems, they can transform themselves into a highly versatile productive force, for the benefit of their family and to the world. Even in the schools the teachers could not pay much attention to set right these misbehaving minds. It is almost by the end of their schooling the mindset of these kids are permanently disabled / spoiled.

Several renowned families have lost their family pride and even their generations because of their rebellious son's or daughter's bad behaviors, attitude and company. The lack of knowledge about bringing up their off springs or lack of attention to their children also fuels this fire. Several of them, fall victims for this ignorance or indifference of these situations over again and again. This order of disorderliness and wrong thinking process is dominating the minds of youngsters. Although many of the them are not offensive, youngsters are exposed to "Forbidden Zones" that could be great hazards for their life and society. The growing crimes and scams are obvious on the daily hot news headlines thru several communication media. In a nut shell the world is becoming so crazy even among the educated society.

My vision is that the scenario has to change and bring in transformation in the minds of younger generations. I just took a step forward to influence the youngsters to make them understand their value of life, and induce the right way of thinking and be successful and productive in their life. This book would certainly help even those have fallen in trap out of situations and willing to recover from bad path and give enough moral strength. I am positive that this book would act as their personal guide and bring the world to a more orderly and righteous place as every holy soul wanted this world to be.

It is like a person with decades of driving experience getting involved in an accident, forgetting to switch on the turn signal before a right turn. Though there are several self-books available in the market, I hope this is going to be unique as I have presented whatever I have come across while conversing with lot of elders and senior friends over a period of time and also through my life long observations . The Life's most essential information for day to day life are presented in the form of hot simple formulae which could be realized by only a few fortunate thru a life time experience. This book has also been structured in the way that the essence of Life's most essential messages given in capsulated form in a most novel and attractive way so that they will directly impact the youngsters and make them realize that they are walking on this mess over and over again but never try to fix all these messes" and thus, eventually bring out phenomenal societal transformation. You can call it as an effective wake up call for the society, in particular to younger generations.

I hope when an elderly person go through every message in this book should say Yes, this is what I wanted to carry on to my daughters, sons and younger generations and wanted them to just follow and would be so glad to present a copy to each of their children or grandchildren. Though I have authored several technical articles, this is my first attempt to author a general book like this for the society. I am presenting my brain child, entitled " *I do not know why it took so much time for me,*" After going thru this book I hope you will feel the importance of the contents and definitely would be happy to present every one you love a copy each.

Dr.Gopal
(Dr.Gopalakrishnan Viswanathan)

ACKNOWLEDGEMENT

It is my sincere thanks for all the elders and my seniors who were great inspiration for me to write this book. My thanks are due for Dr.Srinivasan of Phoenix who first sampled this book and his emotional reaction was key in bringing this book for publication. My heartfelt thanks to Mr.Raghavendra Rao of NASA and Mrs.Durga Rao for their constructive criticism and enthusiasm to publish this book. I want to thank my Parents and Parents in law for their patience and support for me to complete this work. I want to thank my sisters, brothers-in-law and their families. I want to thank my brother in law Mr.Viswanthan Subbarayan for helping in formatting the book per publisher's recommendations. I do want to acknowledge my wife Sivagamasundari and sons Balaji and Siddharth for their patience and support at different stages of my life.

GOD

- To understand that Lord is all Merciful.

- To understand I should never take God's mercy for granted.

- To understand every day is a Gift of God.

- To understand that I can't realize God as long as I Keep debating on Him, But only when I surrender to him.

- To understand what we need is faith in Him and not just belief.

- To understand my relationship with the Lord.

- To understand that God is not in my reach but His mercy is.

- To understand to profoundly thank God for all the resources He has provided me as on the day.

- To understand why God did not give me anything I wanted but just gave me everything I needed.

- To understand my prayers should be like a steering wheel and not like a spare tire.

- **To understand that God's words are announcements and not for debate.**

- **To understand that I should keep all faith on God and Keep working on my duties.**

- **To understand that I should put in my efforts for everything I want to achieve, but once they are achieved, then, leave the laurels to God.**

- **To understand that I should never take God for granted.**

- To understand that the will of God will never take me where the grace of God will not protect me.

- To understand that God is not only helping me to completely live a righteous life, till the tail end but also for a honorable, graceful death.

PARENTS

- To understand that my parents are living God to me.

- To understand that Motherhood is all about Sacrifice.

- To understand that Fatherhood is all about Magnanimity.

- To understand that my Parents are my second source of Mercy, Care Takers and Well-wishers.

- To understand that my parents are my best guides in my life.

- **To understand that I should never take parents and their mercy for granted.**

- **To understand that absolute obedience to my parents is the first step in my life.**

- **To understand that I should observe every etiquette to my parents.**

- **To understand that Love allows me to grow under traits but not to grumble.**

- **To understand that I should be in humble, calm and respectful mood before my parents.**

- To understand that If I do not obey my parents I will have to obey everyone else in this world.

- To understand that I should talk to my parents politely without any anger.

- To understand that why my parents wanted to know where I am going and whom I am hanging around with.

- To understand that my parents and family have abundance of expectations on me.

- To understand that growing under the grace of parents is a matchless experience in my life.

- To understand that I have several reasons to be grateful to my parents.

- To understand that I should obey and help my family system.

- To understand that I should talk with love, courtesy and respect with my family.

- To understand that I should stop blaming others for whatever is happening to me.

- To understand that why my parents did not tell me how to live instead they lived and let me watch them living a righteous life and then let me to start my life.

- To understand that I should do exactly what my parents asked me to do.

- To understand that I should obey right away to my parents directions.

- To understand that what I make will make me.

- To understand that I should be a creature of good habits.

- To understand that a fool will not hesitate to go to places where a wise will dare to go.

- To understand even before I understood my life's purpose, half of my life was lost.

- To understand the urgency of disciplined behavior in my daily life.

- To understand that I should work to keep everything in order, neat and tidy.

- To understand that I should never become slave of bad habits.

- To understand that I should be ready to change for the best.

- **To understand that every kid has the responsibility of making the home a paradise.**

- **To understand that why my parents always used to say, Be Careful.**

SCHOOL/ TEACHER

- To understand to have a firm grasp of, My very purpose of being in the class room.

- To understand while class is on, My mind is wandering and not listening to what the Teacher teaches.

- To understand that we take pride unfortunately in being insubordinate and rebellious.

- To understand that I should never act out of character.

- To understand that I should never take Teachers for granted.

- **To understand I should do what my teacher instructs me to do.**

- **To understand that I should always be receptive for class room teachings.**

- **To understand that I should Observe, listen and learn in my class room.**

- **To understand that I should never be fearful of my studies at the same time learn the subjects with utmost respect.**

- **To understand that school life is all about my self-preparations.**

- **To understand that I should be hungry for knowledge and success in life.**

- **To understand that I should not go to any place, where I do not see any protection.**

- **To understand that I should avoid any trouble creators and distracters at school.**

- **To understand that I should talk politely and respectfully to my Teachers.**

- **To understand that I should keep my curiosity alive for making my learning, an enjoyable experience.**

- To understand that I should be a lifelong learner, and enjoy in self learning.

- To understand that I can spin every day to my advantage with my proper behavior.

- To understand that I should have the sense of urgency in preparing myself for life.

- To understand procrastination should be a forgotten/forbidden word in my life.

- To understand that I need to focus on what I need to do in the world of distractions.

- To understand that I should be a happy warrior as for my study preparations are concerned.

- To understand to exercise my self-control and pay attention to what I am doing.

- To understand that I should develop myself, worthy enough day by day.

- To understand that resting will lead to rusting.

- To understand that life will be interesting to only for those who equip with the best of abilities.

- To understand that I should not live in illusions.

- To understand that we always make big things small and insignificant things big.

- To understand that I should realize my duties ahead of time and complete them with the sense of urgency one by one.

- To understand that If, I had to make my head way, I should focus on my objectives and ignore the distractions.

- To understand even God likes a winner.

- To understand that I should be eating the right kind of just enough food, that will help me in my learning process.

- To Understand while I have to do everything including Paying for monthly bills in time, Why can't I study and prepare myself every now and then.

- To understand that I should constantly strive to, keep cleaning the trashes of thoughts accumulating in my mind and keep it clear.

- To understand when to speak, what to speak and where to speak.

- To understand that I should try hard to get what I like, else I will be forced to accept what I get.

- To understand every kid has the responsibility of making the class and the school a better place.

- To understand that I should stuff myself enough, get on to the stage enact confidently and play my part right and walk out calmly.

- To understand that I should respect my employer, work place and work together with the co-workers to make everyday productive.

PERSONAL

- To understand my improvement is based on my attitude and behavior.

- To understand that I should be self-propeller under the guidance of my parents and teachers.

- To understand if I had listened to all the advices I was offered, I would have never got anything done.

- To understand that when I feel more attractive to myself, I will be much more attractive to others.

- To understand people won't believe in what I say but go with whatever I do and what I have done.

- To understand that I have to get profited from my past experiences.

- To understand that I will never be in trouble for speaking truth.

- To understand I should always develop the acumen and urge to scale the never reached heights.

- To understand that, It is easy to go along with the crowd, but the crowd never goes anywhere that is interesting and helpful.

- **To understand that my responsibilities will keep accumulating on day to day basis like trash, If I do not keep clearing them then and there.**

- **To understand that my efforts should be time sensitive.**

- **To understand that I should have a firm grasp on what I need.**

- **To understand that I should avoid irresponsible and careless talks.**

- **To understand that, If can I control my flow of thoughts in mind I could avoid my day in fact life, ending up with regrettable notes.**

- To understand that mostly, I am the problem creator for myself.

- To understand If, I do not work for it, I will not get it.

- To understand that I should not have bad surprises in my life, as they are stressful and difficult to handle.

- To understand that I should make whatever adjustments I needed to make myself for achieving my goals.

- To understand always I should look for a way to make myself a better person.

- **To understand what got me here, won't get me there.**

- **To understand that Indecisiveness and Inaction are indices of my personal disability.**

- **To understand my limits of enjoyment.**

- **To understand that when it comes to our personal life there is no margin for error.**

- **To understand that I should free myself from emotional traps.**

- To understand a good sense of humor helps me to overcome my obstacles in getting things done.

- To understand I should empower myself with all the skills of life.

- To understand that I should always be prepared for any Indecisive phase in my life.

- To understand that I should remain stable in a constantly changing world and keep moving in a still, stagnated and frozen world.

- To understand I do not have to be perfect in all my attempts, all it counts is my participation.

- To succeed in a system I should plug myself in to the system.

- To understand that life is not an 8a.m to 5p.m affair.

- To understand that I should get out of my world and explore the mysteries of the world, to learn new things.

- To understand the rough patch I am going thru now will become a wrinkle in the long run.

- To understand that I am wasting my time on several unwanted things.

- To understand that I should avoid irresponsible and careless talks.

- To understand what I make, Will make me.

- To understand that I can customize my life according to my needs and interests.

- To understand that I should not always think about my failures and weaknesses.

- To understand challenge and Prospects coexists.

- To understand that the future will follow the brave.

- To understand that I should conquer my slackness, lethargy, and procrastination, carelessness and inattentiveness which are the most serious attributes that make me to struggle all thru my life.

- To understand that I should gain a deep understanding of the problems plaguing me.

- To understand that I should work, without any confusions.

- To understand the urgency of disciplined behavior.

- To understand that, I should, keep pace with change.

- To understand that my old habits are like warm blanket, I would never want to throw.

- To understand speaking without thinking is not safe and good.

- To understand my foolish words will create me, hundreds of enemies.

- To understand, Only when I raise up for my cause and start working, I will realize all the resistance and pains in reaching the goals.

- To understand that I should think steadily and act swiftly.

- To understand that I should plan my work and work on my plan.

- To understand that my drive for the success should be in the fast lane.

- To understand you can beat the world if you can beat the clock.

- To understand that I should have an organized work culture.

- To understand that I can keep working on myself to improve my capabilities.

- To understand that fear of defeat is worse than the actual downfall.

- To understand that many victories are worse than a defeat.

- To understand that If I can keep celebrating my mind I can even change a defeat in to a victory.

- To understand that, If I can control my emotions during my victory I am entitled for a second victory.

- **To understand that faith makes things possible, not easy.**

- **To understand a person is created by his hurdles and not by the help.**

- **To understand it is impossible to win this world using bad tricks.**

- **To understand the secret of success is working hard and not worrying about the problem.**

- **To understand that nothing is easy if you do not want to do it and nothing is difficult if you want to do it.**

- To understand that I am loosing myself when I am in anger.

- To understand that there is nothing more attractive than a happy positive person.

- To understand that respect is not a gift, I should earn it.

- To understand that it is integrity to keep up the promised word, while it is intelligence to be more careful while promising a word.

- To understand that we should work restlessly for our life.

- **To understand that the duties neglected by us will deliver the truth that we failed to understand.**

- **To understand that a genius will light up his own intellect.**

- **To understand success is never final and failure is never fatal.**

- **To understand that I can share only my joy, but to keep and lock my fears within myself.**

- **To understand that Unknowns are not good.**

- To understand that one who knows the world will not feel shy and one who knows himself will not be proud.

- To understand for a Wise, Life is an ongoing stream of problems, while a fool wants the life to be a finished chapter.

- To understand that I need not be loyal to my wishes and friends but I should be loyal to my parents and studies / job.

- To understand that the anger I burst outside will lead to forgiveness, while the anger I tried to hide would lead to enmity and catastrophe.

- **To understand that I misunderstood Laziness for patience.**

- **To understand that Success is relative, more success more relatives.**

- **To understand that Life if full of promises for me to prove.**

NEIGHBORS

& SOCIETY

- To understand that I should talk to my neighbors with love and respect.

- To understand that I have to behave responsibly since the society always monitors me.

- To understand Happiness and Sadness are purely my choice.

- To understand that imposing restrictions on ourselves is not fun, but it is the best way to build the values.

- To understand under any given situation I should focus on facts and not on emotions.

- To understand that hopes and wishes should guide me and not fear.

- To understand only happy people can make others happy.

- To understand that how to make every day productive and exciting.

- To understand to adopt myself for the changing demand.

- To understand that I should always have better relationship with neighbors.

- To understand that neighbors are my second family away from my home.

PROFESSION

OR

WORK

❧

- To understand that I should be always helpful to my company and my boss.

- To understand that I should never talk anything against my company or coworkers.

- To understand that to keep thinking I should work hard and achieve things maximum I could, than to always thinking of holidays and food and rest.

- To understand that an intelligent will know to pass on a message at the correct time, while a wise knows whether to pass on the message or not.

- To understand that the number of forces working against you is a proof of levels of success.

- To understand that First I should deserve then I can desire.

- To understand that we consider others are fools when we do not understand or envy others.

- To understand that most of them get tired while chasing the retirement.

- To understand that the first step of victory is being more enthusiastic about the job.

- To understand that when we point out someone else for our failures, We start losing all our victories.

- To understand that I should be submissive before those who give me freedom.

- To understand that every individual has the responsibility of making the work place a better one.

WHEN I AM YOUNG

❧

- To understand that mistakenly I believe, I know everything.

- To understand that I believe everything is going to happen according to my wish.

- To understand that I believe by default that my parents and teachers should listen to me.

- To understand that I believe in challenging every one or arguing with every one.

- To understand that I believe people interested in my life should walk away, while people who want to take me for granted are helpful and good.

- To understand that I believe by default the graceful situations will continue forever and never think, plan and put my efforts towards my tasks and future.

- To understand that I believe and like avoiding my parents, teachers and studies on day to day basis instead of consulting them and discussing about What I am doing, my problems and for a plan, what I am supposed to do.

- To understand that I should keep myself calm and undisturbed by any entity I might encounter at every instant of my life so as to perform my duties efficiently at its best.

- To understand that I have to be armored with all good manners, discipline, habits, drive, efforts, … before I step up in to this world.

- To understand that all the directions and advices from my parents were only in the interest of my wellbeing and not to suppress my happiness.

- To understand that Never get attracted to other impulsive attractions which are only just traps for your valuable life.

- **To understand that I should have a well spent and accomplished life.**

- **To understand that Life is like walking with a candle light through a hall of gun powder. So I should be wise and have discretions.**

WHEN

I AM

OLD

- **To understand, In my life nothing will be happening in accordance to my wishes but only per Lord's will.**

- **To understand that, I have to work and put my efforts for my survival and progress.**

- **To understand that I should have done everything early and ASAP.**

- **To understand that I should never look around others and wasting time rather focus on my progress.**

- **To understand that my humility and my own responsible behavior are going to take me safe every day and make me happy.**

- **To understand that keeping my body and mind healthy and away from bad habits and bad thinking process is essential for my survival.**

- **To understand that I have to make sure I will never fall in hands of bad people or trouble.**

- **To understand that I should have focused only on my duties and my family progress rather than everything else.**

- **To understand to feel the urgency of disciplining myself and achieving my targets in life.**

- **To understand that Great Minds will have purpose and the rest will have only desire.**

- **To understand that when it comes to life there is no margin for error.**

- **To understand that the world do not bother about the number of hurricanes you have encountered in your life journey, but only want to know if you could sail the ship safe to the port.**

- **To understand life is like a bundle of rope, when it is closer to the end, faster it will go.**

- **To understand that everything is fun till it happen to us.**

- **To understand why everyone neglects me even when I offer my full support to anyone.**

- **To understand why I should have had the habit of keeping my body fit, for which I should have practiced from younger days.**

- **To understand why I should not have got in to any vices.**

- If the Lord had provided me everything I wanted, I would have destroyed myself.

- To understand that I should not have to accept all the societal disorientations and misconducts in the name of civilization advancement.

- To understand that I do not have to go through rigorous experiences and pay heavy penalties to behave responsibly in life.